DEGAS / LAUTREC

Degas/Lautrec

Text and Notes by
KEITH ROBERTS

TUDOR PUBLISHING COMPANY
New York

TUDOR PUBLISHING COMPANY

New York, 1967

Library of Congress Catalog Card Number: 67-19842

Printed in Japan

DEGAS AND LAUTREC
PAINTERS OF PARISIAN LIFE

Degas and Toulouse-Lautrec belong to a great period of French art, and without them painting in France in the second half of the nineteenth century would have lost an element not only of its greatness but also of its variety. They have become "Old Masters" and the aura of familiarity, admiration and great value that surrounds their work has made it additionally hard to appreciate the degree to which, in choice of themes and their treatment, they were avant-garde in their time. But though often scorned and criticized, they had sufficient private means to be able to ignore the more conventional sources of patronage. Although something like a fifth of his work consists of portraits, Degas probably never accepted a formal commission. Both painters could count on the support of only a small circle of discerning collectors and such sympathetic dealers as Vollard and Durand-Ruel.

Both were brilliant draughtsmen and in their work they emphasized line. The movements of the human figure, for its own sake, and as indications of character and personality, were their prime concern; and they did not share the general Impressionist interest in landscape, though they did, in fact, paint them (cf. Plates 42 and 49). They were artists of the city and created unforgettable images of Parisian life. *Brilliant draughtsmen*

At heart Degas and Lautrec were unhappy men but they learned early to conceal their vulnerability and loneliness behind an armory of mordant wit. And in the end both were tragically defeated by physical liabilities. Lautrec died of the combined effects of syphilis, alcohol and general excess at the age of thirty-seven. Degas lived to be eighty-three, but the last twenty-five

5

years of his life were an agony to him because of his failing sight, which hindered him from engaging in the only pursuit that gave him any real pleasure.

But although a great deal links the two artists, there are perhaps even more factors, by way of temperament, character, circumstance, upbringing and achievement, that separate them. And at bottom, a generation intervened between their births, and it was a generation of vast importance in art history.

Edgar de Gas (later contracted by the artist to Degas) was born in Paris on July 19, 1834, the eldest of five children. His mother belonged to a French family that had settled in New Orleans. His father, a banker, was a man of considerable culture, devoted to music, opera and the theatre, and though he obliged Edgar to study law for a short time, he did not create any serious obstacles when his son asked to be allowed to take up painting.

In 1852, Degas was allowed to transform a room in the family home in the rue Mondivi into a studio, and during the following year began to work under Félix-Joseph Barrias. Much of his time was also spent copying Old Masters in the Louvre and studying the prints of Dürer, Mantegna, Goya and Rembrandt. In 1854, he studied with Louis Lamothe, an ardent disciple of Ingres, the greatest living exponent of the classical style.

In 1855, Degas entered the Ecole des Beaux-Arts, but soon found the course unprofitable and the regime too restricting. To study the classical tradition at its source seemed altogether more profitable. As he had hospitable relatives in Florence and Naples, he was able to make long and regular trips to Italy in the years 1854–9. He studied hard, painting copies of Italian pictures he admired and filling sketchbooks with further copies, compositions and precepts.

In April, 1859, he took a studio in the rue Madame in Paris, and began to concentrate on portraits and historical subjects. Of these early portraits, *The Bellelli Family* (Plate 4) is the grandest and most important, and illustrates some of the artist's most

6

fundamental characteristics. The first impression is of monumentality, calm and order. And it is, perhaps, only after prolonged study that one begins to appreciate the unusual features of the painting. For the apparent austerity of the grouping is equalled by its contrived casualness. The central figure is not, as one might expect, the head of the house, but the younger daughter wearing an ordinary pinafore.

Similar qualities are to be found in the beautiful portrait of Hortense Valpinçon (Plate 9). Again, though to a greater degree, there is the suggestion of everyday life. It is as if the little girl eating her apple had quite suddenly been asked in the middle of the afternoon to look in the artist's direction for a moment while he painted her portrait. The implicit contradiction is extremely significant. What Degas wanted to do was to capture the spontaneity of life, but without any loss of artistic strictness. Always at the back of his mind was a precise arrangement of line and color that would combine what he most admired in the classical tradition, firmness and inevitability of design, with a vivid sense of contemporary life. He expressed his aims in characteristically epigrammatic fashion when he wrote in an early notebook: "Ah, Giotto, don't prevent me from seeing Paris; and, Paris, don't prevent me from seeing Giotto."

It was this consciousness of a twin obligation that led Degas to see in apparently trivial events, a woman drying her feet (Plate 33), perhaps, or a laundress yawning (Plate 35), artistic possibilities of an heroic order—just as it led him to depict classical scenes with a new informality. *The Young Spartans* (Plate 3) amounts, really, to a series of studies of the adolescent nude. There is little sense of an historic context. Degas had a great admiration for the art of the past, and scant respect for progress, but at the same time he began to see the difficulties of history painting. The whole spirit of the nineteenth century, with its materialism, literal emphasis and stress on scientific examination, was destroying the delicate balance between imagination and fact

"The Young Spartans"

7

on which for centuries the whole success of history painting had depended. In 1866 Degas abandoned the painting of historical subjects.

It was a crucial decision in which a number of other factors were also involved. In 1862, he had met the painter Manet, who was becoming increasingly interested in themes from modern life. About this time, he also met a friend of Manet's named Edmond Duranty, a critic and novelist who was anxious to break down the barrier that he felt had for too long existed between art and life. Degas soon became a familiar figure at the Café Guerbois, where many of the artists associated with the development of Impressionism were accustomed to meet and talk in the evening.

But even though Degas gave up historical subjects, he did not forgo any of the disciplines associated with the classical tradition of history painting. "No art is less spontaneous than mine," he once remarked to George Moore. "What I do is the result of reflection and study of the great masters; of inspiration, spontaneity, temperament, I know nothing." This relationship to the art of the past is one of the essential differences between Degas

Differ-
ences
from
Lautrec

and Toulouse-Lautrec. Lautrec had little feeling for the tradition of Raphael and Poussin; he liked experiment and novelty. Degas burrowed deep but left on his work an anonymous stamp. Renoir once compared his nudes to the Parthenon sculptures; and all his figures have that sense of being individual but, at the same time, impersonal, which is a hallmark of so much antique art. Just as he said that he wanted to be famous but unknown, Degas did not wish "to get personal" in his art.

Lautrec was always more direct. Even a conventional study of the nude like *Fat Maria* (Plate 52) establishes a degree of involvement with the model that Degas—a very reserved man— was always at pains to avoid, just as he avoided those intimate glimpses into personal relationships that Lautrec found so fasci-

Lautrec

nating (cf. Plates 65, 77, 83, 86). Both artists wished to create an impression of the flux of life, but whereas Degas was pri-

8

marily interested in the pictorial side, at the expense of the figures' identities, Lautrec, moving in a raffish milieu which was easily bored and always on the lookout for new faces, came to create at the same time images of the "passing parade." He painted the singers and dancers of the Parisian music-halls and cabarets: Jane Avril, "La Goulue," Valentin-le-Désossé, Loïe Fuller, Yvette Guilbert, et al., and invariably, it is interesting to note, at the height of their often short-lived fame.

These differences in their art reflect the great differences in temperament and character between the two men. Lautrec was born at Albi on November 24, 1864, and was christened Henri-Marie-Raymond de Toulouse-Lautrec Monfa. His family was aristocratic and rich, though by no means united. His father, Comte Alphonse, was constantly unfaithful to his wife, and, what was perhaps even more trying, extremely eccentric. The cynicism that was to mark Lautrec's relations with women, and his complete disregard for convention may have been influenced by this, but they also had deeper roots in his experiences as a child. As a youth, Lautrec delighted his father—a keen sportsman—with his own enthusiasm for riding and hunting. He admired physical abilities, and his health was in general fairly good, although he was of small stature. In 1878, however, he broke his left leg and, in the following year, the right. The bones did not mend properly, with the result that while Lautrec developed the torso of a fully grown man, his legs were stunted. He was to all intents and purposes a dwarf. *Lautrec —family back- ground*

Forced to give up his favorite sports, he turned to art for consolation. He had already revealed a natural aptitude for sketching, and, in 1881, began to take proper drawing lessons from René Princeteau, an animal painter from Bordeaux who was a friend of the family. Princeteau advised Lautrec's parents to allow their son to study in Paris under Bonnat, a famous academic painter of the day. Lautrec enrolled in the studio in 1882; but soon afterwards Bonnat decided to give up teaching. Lautrec remained in *Early training*

9

Paris—which was to be the center of his activities right up to his death—and went on to study with Corman. His early works were attractive but fairly conventional (cf. Plates 49–52), and in the early 1880s he was still looking forward to the day when he would gain official honors. But he had reckoned without one vital factor: Montmartre.

Mont-martre

Lautrec's physical stature made him exceptionally neurotic and though he might take every care to conceal it, highly sensitive. With its free and easy ways, Montmartre satisfied his need for a milieu in which he could come and go, if not unnoticed, at least in an atmosphere of friendly tolerance. Montmartre also provided the painter with a steady stream of more or less dubious women, from one of whom he contracted the syphilis that helped to kill him. Like most "picturesque" quarters in cosmopolitan cities, Montmartre boasted its freaks, outcasts and human derelicts. Lautrec, himself a freak, was fascinated by what was monstrous, *outré* and unconventional, and it is this bias which subtly permeated his work and gives his paintings and posters their particular flavor, at once fascinating and faintly repellent. Examining an unflattering sketch that he had made of her, Yvette Guilbert remarked, "Really, Henri, you're a genius at distorting." "But of course," he replied. The words, Yvette records, had the sting of a lash.

Montmartre was also the haunt of many of the avant-garde artists of the day. Contact with painters and exposure to both the pictures and the ideas they embodied soon led Lautrec away from the conventional path. At the same time, he did not become a slavish follower of novelty. His aristocratic upbringing, for one thing, had instilled in him too strong a spirit of independence for that. Some of his early work (e.g., Plate 51) reveals the influence of Impressionism; but he never really developed any great interest in one of the keys to Impressionist style, the rendering of sunlight. Lautrec is always at his best when the light is artificial.

From 1887, Lautrec began to exhibit regularly in group exhibitions, such as the *Société des XX* in Paris and Brussels, the *Salon des Indépendants*, the *Cercle Volney* and the *Arts Libéraux*. His work also began to appear in various periodicals, *Courrier Français*, *Paris Illustré*, *Figaro Illustré*, *Rire*, etc. In 1888, he produced his first really independent picture, *The Cirque Fernando* (Plate 54), in which he adopted, and in the process made his own, many of the stylistic devices already used by Degas, the painter whom he revered above all others.

"The Cirque Fernando"

Degas's pictures had begun to reflect his changing views some time before, in the second half of the 1860s, when he had turned for inspiration not to the classical authors but to the race-course (cf. Plate 10) and the theatre. He continued to exhibit at the official Paris Salon until 1870. In the Franco-Prussian War, he served in the artillery; and it was due to a severe chill contracted during military service that his eyes first began to give him trouble.

Between October, 1872, and April, 1873, Degas was in America, visiting his brothers in New Orleans. On his return, he settled in a studio in the rue Blanche and concentrated on themes from modern life, often connected with some professional skill: dancers (e.g., Plates 11, 14, 18), singers (Plates 16, 19), acrobats (Plate 26), musicians (Plate 8), milliners (Plate 32), washerwomen (Plate 21), and laundresses (Plate 35). To this list he soon added the female nude which became, with the dancers, his favorite subject matter in later years.

Degas— new themes

Degas contributed ten works—dancers, race scenes, and studies of a washerwoman and a female nude—to the group show mounted by the Impressionists in 1874; and he exhibited at all the others, save that of 1882. In 1881, he showed *The Dancer Dressed* (one of the bronze casts in the Tate Gallery, London), the only one of his sculptures exhibited during his lifetime. After 1886, the date of the eighth and last Impressionist exhibition, Degas stopped sending in his works to public exhibitions. His eyesight was by now poor and he worked increasingly in pastel, a medium with two distinct advantages. It was susceptible to bolder effects than oils, and in this sense was easier to work, and it enabled him to retain color without sacrificing line. In the later years, Degas found an outlet for his frustrated talents in photography, posing and lighting his friends in strict accordance with the principles he had evolved in his painting.

The Japanese print

Degas had always been interested in photography; it had, indeed, been one of the important influences on the development of his style. Another influence in working out pictorial formulae that would accommodate the fragmentary vision of life in which he was so interested was the Japanese print, which had become both popular and fashionable in the early 1860s. From the colorful prints of Japan, he learned how to cut off the figure abruptly (e.g., on the right in Plate 18), how to achieve effects through calculated asymmetry in the composition (e.g., Plates 10 and 29), the advantages of the unusual viewpoint (e.g., Plates 23 or 26) as well as a bold use of the close-up (e.g., Plate 24). The sloping foregrounds (e.g., Plates 18, 29), however, and unusual sight angles were probably suggested by photographs.

Many of these devices Toulouse-Lautrec now took over in his own work; and several of them are to be found in *The Cirque Fernando*. There is the same rather unusual view-point (see also Plates 57 and 63), the same somewhat flattened space, and figures are cut off by the frame in a similar way. Peculiar to Lautrec himself, however, is the element of caricature—in the ringmaster, for example—and the use of bold, simplified, essentially non-naturalistic color. The picture already has, in fact, almost all the elements Lautrec was to exploit in his posters. He made his first lithographic print, a poster for the Moulin Rouge, in 1891; and altogether he made 400 prints in black and white and in color, as well as 31 posters proper. Lautrec was among the first and, in some ways, the greatest of poster designers. He had flair, panache, the right sense of exaggeration; and in posters his

Lautrec —posters

feeling for life as a charade could find a perfect outlet. It is also important to remember that he was, so to say, on the spot at the right moment, when the naturalism of the Impressionists was in decline. In their rejection of the naturalistic mode, Lautrec's posters—and, indeed, most of his paintings as well—express the stylistic preoccupations of the late 1880s and nineties as clearly as the pictures of Seurat or Gauguin. One of the crucial differences between Lautrec and Degas is that Degas's art had its roots in the formative period of Impressionism, while that of Lautrec is a product of its later, "Mannerist" phase.

Lautrec's life became more and more dissipated as the nineties wore on. The quality and the quantity of his work slowly declined, though he had every incentive to improve both. Fakes were already in circulation in the middle of the decade. Finally, in 1899, he had a complete mental and physical breakdown and was confined to a sanitarium. He resumed work while still an inmate, partly to prove his sanity, and on his release took up painting again, though now in a somewhat different style. In Lautrec's late work (Plates 86–90) there is less emphasis on line, the strokes are richer, broader, more emphatic; and the coloring is more somber. The physical inability to draw lines with the old precision may have had a good deal to do with this change. And certainly Lautrec did not survive for very long. Surrounded by his family, he died on September 9, 1901. The contents of his studio were carefully preserved and later presented to the town of Albi.

The last twenty years of Degas's life were wretched. His eyesight deteriorated still further in the 1890s; while in the early years of the new century he could only work, and then with difficulty, on large compositions or sculpture. Finally, in 1908, he more or less gave up art altogether. For a man who had never been particularly happy and who had concentrated on painting to the virtual exclusion of everything else (he never married), the blow was crippling. Degas's life was over. But he went on

13

living, occasionally his old self but more often than not morose and irritable, repeating his old maxims and anecdotes and falling into terrible silences that he would break with the single, pathetic pronouncement: "Death is all I think of."

In 1912, eviction from his home in the rue Victor Massé caused Degas further anguish. A new studio was found for him; but he never really settled there. He took to wandering the streets aimlessly, and was often in danger of being run over. On more than one occasion he was compared, "in his Inverness cape, tapping his cane, feeling his way," to the blind Homer, or Lear deprived of his daughters. Famous and revered, Degas died in Paris in September, 1917. The contents of his studio were dispersed in a number of sales in Paris in 1918.

Further Reading

DEGAS

Boggs, Jean Sutherland: *Portraits by Degas*. University of California Press, 1962.

Browse, Lillian: *Degas Dancers*. Faber, London, 1949.

Cooper, Douglas: *Pastels by Edgar Degas*. Collier-Macmillan, London, 1954.

Rewald, John: *Degas' Sculpture*. Abrams, New York, 1957.

TOULOUSE-LAUTREC

Mack, Gerstle: *Toulouse-Lautrec*. Jonathan Cape, London, 1938.

Cooper, Douglas: *Toulouse-Lautrec*. Thames & Hudson, London, 1955.

Perruchot, Henri: *Toulouse-Lautrec*. Perpetua Books, London, 1960.

Sutton, Denys: *Lautrec*. Paul Hamlyn, London, 1962.

TABLE OF DATES

Edgar Degas

1834   Edgar Degas born in Paris on July 19th. The father's family was Breton, but had left France during the Revolution and settled in Naples. The mother's family had also left France during the Revolution and settled in New Orleans. The family name was "de Gas" but Degas himself changed the form.

1845–52   At school, at the Lycée Louis le Grand.

1852–4   Begins to study art on a full time basis, under Barrias and Lamothe.

1854–9   Regular visits to Italy, where he studies Renaissance and Antique art.

1859   (April) Takes a studio in the rue Madame, Paris, and concentrates on portraiture and historical subjects.

1865–70   Contributes regularly to the official Salon. By 1865, however, he has already met Whistler, Fantin Latour, Renoir, Manet, Monet and Sisley.

1870   Serves in the Franco-Prussian war. By this date, he is already interested in such "modern" subjects as the theatre and horses and riders.

1872–3   Visits his brothers in New Orleans and paints several pictures there.

1874   Contributes to the first Impressionist Exhibition in Paris (as he will to all the others with the exception of the 1882 show).

1880   Visit to Spain.

1886   Contributes to the last of the Impressionist Exhibitions. After this date ceases to send his work to public exhibitions, though they are shown commercially by Durand-Ruel, the dealer. By this date, Degas is working more and more in pastel.

1889   Visits Spain with the painter Boldini.

1905   Exhibition of Impressionists organized by Durand-Ruel at the Grafton Galleries in London. *The Times* critic singles out Degas for attack.

1911   Becomes an Honorary Member of the Royal Scottish Academy.

1912   By this date Degas has become famous and his works relatively popular. *La Danseuse à la Barre* (New York, Metropolitan Museum), in fact, fetches about $100,000 (450,000 francs) at auction.

1917   September 27. Dies in Paris, and is buried in the family tomb at the Montmarte cemetery.

Henri Toulouse-Lautrec

1864   November 24th Henri-Marie-Raymond de Toulouse-Lautrec Monfa born in the Hotel du Bosc, the family house at Albi. His father was Comte Alphonse and his mother, a first cousin of her husband's, Adele Tapié de Céleyran.

1872   The family moves to Paris, where Henri goes to school at the Lycée Fontanes. Here he meets Maurice Joyant, who was to remain one of his most devoted friends.

1878   The family returns to Albi, where Henri continues his education with his mother. He falls on a slippery floor and breaks his left leg.

1879   Lautrec now breaks his right femur; he remains an invalid; and is obliged to give up his favorite sports, riding and shooting.

1881	His formal education ceases when he passes the first part of his *baccalauréat*. Takes his first formal drawing lessons with René Princeteau, an animal painter.
1882	On Princeteau's advice, he enrolls in Bonnat's studio in Paris, but only stays there a short time because Bonnat decides to abandon teaching. Continues his studies under Cormon.
1880s	Becomes increasingly tied to Montmartre, where he finds his subjects, models, friends and mistresses. Becomes friendly (1885) with the singer Bruant, and first shows his paintings in public on the walls of Bruant's cabaret, "Le Mirliton."
1887	From 1887 Lautrec's work is widely shown in group exhibitions: the *Société des XX* (Paris and Brussels), the *Salon des Indépendants,* the *Cercle Volney,* the *Arts Libéraux,* etc. Lautrec also works for periodicals, such as *Rire, Figaro Illustré, Courrier Français* and *Paris Illustré.*
1891	Makes his first lithographic print with a poster for the Moulin Rouge. And during the early 1890s, paints many pictures of the dance halls and of the stars who appeared there. Also begins to work in brothels, often living in them for days on end.
1893	Holds his first important exhibition with Charles Maurin at the Boussod-Valadon Gallery in Paris.
1894	Visits London with Maurice Joyant. Publishes an album of his lithographs devoted to the diseuse-Yvette Guilbert.
1899	At the end of February, he suffers a complete collapse and is taken to a sanatorium at Neuilly, where he remains until May. While undergoing treatment, he makes a series of drawings from memory of circus subjects. After leaving the sanatorium, he begins painting again. Stays at le Crotoy, le Havre, Arcachon, Bordeaux.
1901	Attempts to resume his old way of life, but even though only in his mid-thirties, whoring and drinking have taken their toll. In August, he arrives at Malromé to visit his mother. On September 9th he dies.

LIST OF COLOR PLATES

EDGAR DEGAS

1. Self Portrait in a Green Vest. 1855–6.
2. Still-Life. c. 1858–60.
3. The Young Spartans. 1860.
4. The Bellelli Family. 1858–62.
5. Thérèse de Gas. c. 1863.
6. Study of a Young Woman. c. 1867.
7. Study of Hands. 1858–62.
8. Auguste de Gas Listening to Pagans. 1869–72.
9. Hortense Valpinçon. c. 1870.
10. Carriage at the Races. c. 1870–73.
11. The Dance Foyer at the Opera, Rue le Peletier. 1872.
12. The Rehearsal. c. 1873.
13. Girls Combing their Hair. 1875–6.
14. Dancer (*detail from* The Rehearsal). 1875.
15. Women at a Café: Evening. c. 1877.
16. Café Concert: "The Song of the Dog." 1875–7.
17. Harlequin and Colombine. c. 1884.
18. The Rehearsal. 1873–4.
19. Café-Concert des Ambassadeurs. 1876–7.
20. L'Absinthe. 1876.
21. Two Laundresses. 1876–8.
22. The Ballet Class. c. 1878.
23. Dancer on the Stage. 1878.
24. The Café Singer. 1878.
25. The Curtain Falls. 1880.
26. Miss La La at the Cirque Fernando. 1879.
27. Portrait of Diego Martelli. 1879.
28. The Dancer's Dressing Room. 1879.
29. At the Races. 1877-80.
30. Dancer Leaving her Dressing Room. c. 1881.
31. Waiting. c. 1882.
32. At the Milliner's. c. 1885.
33. After the Bath. 1883.
34. Singer in Green. 1884.
35. Laundresses. c. 1884.
36. Dancers on Stage, Seen from a Box. 1885.
37. Miss Cassatt at the Louvre. 1880.
38. Hélène Rouart. 1886.
39. The Tub. 1886.
40. Dancers at the Bar. c. 1900–5.
41. Dancers in Blue. c. 1890.
42. Lake with Mountains. c. 1890–93.
43. Two Dancers. c. 1898.
44. Horses in Training. c. 1894.
45. Russian Dancers. 1895.
46. Dancers. c. 1899.
47. Woman Drying Herself. c. 1903.

48. Self Portrait. 1880.
49. The Dog-Cart. 1880.
50. The Falconer. 1881.
51. Young Routy. 1882.
52. "Fat Maria." 1894.
53. Vincent van Gogh. 1887.
54. Cirque Fernando: The Equestrienne. 1888.
55. The Laundress. 1889.
56. At the Moulin Rouge: The Dance. 1890.
57. At the Nouveau Cirque: Five Stuffed Shirts. 1891.
58. Last Crumbs (A la Mie). 1891.
59. At the Moulin Rouge. 1892.
60. At the Moulin Rouge: Preparing for the Quadrille. 1892.
61. Jane Avril Leaving the Moulin Rouge. 1892.
62. La Goulue Entering the Moulin Rouge. 1892.
63. The Ballet "Papa Chrysanthème." 1892.
64. A Corner of a Dance Hall. 1892–3.
65. The Kiss. 1892.
66. M. Boileau in a Café. 1893.
67. Jane Avril Dancing. c. 1893.
68. Woman Pulling on her Stockings. 1894.
69. Yvette Guilbert. 1894.

70. The Laundryman Calling at the Brothel. 1894.
71. The Salon in the Rue des Moulins. 1894.
72. Rue des Moulins: the Inspection. 1894.
73. Gabriel Tapié de Céleyran. 1894.
74. Alfred la Guigne. 1894.
75. Miss May Belfort. 1895.
76. La Goulue Dancing (detail). 1895.
77. Friends. 1895.
78. Marcelle Lender Dancing the Boléro in "Chilpéric." 1895–6.
79. Detail of Plate 78.
80. At the Moulin Rouge: the Clowness Cha-U-Kao. 1895.
81. Maxime Dethomas at the Opera Ball. 1896.
82. Woman at her Toilet. 1896.
83. A Box at the Theatre. 1896–7.
84. Portrait of Berthe Bady. 1897.
85. Nude in Front of a Mirror. 1897.
86. In a Private Room at the Rat Mort. 1899.
87. The Barmaid. 1899.
88. Woman at her Toilet: Mme Poupoule. 1900 (?).
89. An Examination at the Faculty of Medicine, Paris. 1901.
90. "Messalina." 1900–1901.

NOTES ON THE COLOR PLATES

EDGAR DEGAS (1834–1917). Plates 1–47.

"L.***" refers to Paul-André Lemoisne's monumental catalogue raisonné of Degas's paintings and pastels (plus some colored drawings). The first four volumes were published in Paris 1946–9. Projected volumes on the drawings have not yet appeared.

1. *Self Portrait in a Green Vest.* Oil on paper applied to canvas. 1855–6. Nepveu-Degas family collection. Although painted when Degas was still a very young man, this self portrait is without any of the romantic bravura with which artists often see themselves in their youth (e.g., Rembrandt or Courbet). L. 11.

2. *Still-Life.* Oil on paper applied to canvas. c. 1858–60. Private Collection, New York. In the second half of the 1850s, Degas made a number of studies, sometimes after Old Masters, or in the life class and, occasionally (as here) of still-life. These were all more or less experimental. Degas was testing his powers. On the reverse, there is another oil study, of a man examining an engraving. This was done much later, however, about 1881. L. 58.

3. *The Young Spartans.* Oil on canvas. 1860. National Gallery, London. In ancient Sparta, it was the custom for boys and girls to exercise and play games together. This work cost the artist a good deal of trouble; and he made many preparatory sketches, as well as two other full size versions. His original conception was much more idealized. There was a temple in the background and the girls were given pure, classical profiles. But in this, the final version, Degas attempted to reconcile the theme with his own visual experience. The girls have the snub noses of Montmartre models. It was Degas's keen sense of actuality which finally made it impossible for him to go on painting traditional academic themes, which he abandoned in 1866. L. 70.

4. *The Bellelli Family*. Oil on canvas. 1858–62. Louvre, Paris. The most ambitious of Degas's early works and one which shows clearly his aim to reconcile classical precision of design with an impression of spontaneity and even casualness—the central figure, after all, is not the head of the family but his younger daughter. Laura de Gas (1814–1897) was the sister of Degas's father; and she married Baron Gennaro Bellelli (1812–1864) in 1842. Giovanna (born 1849) and Giulia (born 1851) Bellelli were thus Degas's cousins. L. 79.

5. *Thérèse de Gas*. Oil on canvas. c. 1863. Louvre, Paris. Degas was a great admirer and, later, owner of Ingres' portraits. And like Ingres, he was concerned with the problem of combining a monumental composition with correct details of contemporary costume. Thérèse (1840–1897) was one of the painter's younger sisters; she married her cousin, Edmondo Morbilli, in Paris in 1863. L. 109.

6. *Study of a Young Woman*. Oil on canvas. c. 1867. Louvre, Paris. Degas already reveals a characteristically Impressionist interest in light. The identity of the sitter is not known. L. 163.

7. *Study of Hands*. Oil on canvas. 1858–62. Louvre, Paris. One of many studies for *The Bellelli Family* (Plate 4). After the artist's death, the contents of the studio were dispersed in three sales in Paris in 1918. This study was in the third sale. L. 181.

8. *Auguste de Gas Listening to Pagans*. Oil on canvas. 1869–72. Museum of Fine Arts, Boston. Degas's father (1807–1874) was extremely fond of music and often held musical evenings. Pagans was a well known Spanish tenor and guitarist and was a welcome guest on such occasions. He was also a familiar figure at Manet's musical evenings. L. 257.

9. *Hortense Valpinçon*. Oil on canvas. c. 1870. Minneapolis Institute of Arts. Hortense Valpinçon was the daughter of Degas's childhood friend, Paul Valpinçon. In its sense of spontaneity, this portrait marks an advance over

Plate 4. The child leans casually against a table; and she seems to turn towards the spectator in a perfunctory manner, as though half her attention is still on the apple she is in the middle of eating. L. 206.

10. *Carriage at the Races.* Oil on canvas. c. 1870–73. Museum of Fine Arts, Boston. Degas appreciated that a naturalistic effect depended not merely on details but, more important still, on the basic structure of the composition. Note how the horses and the bottom of the carriage are cut by the edges of the picture. This device, which Degas took over from Japanese prints, creates an impression of objects and figures unposed, like a snapshot. L. 281.

11. *The Dance Foyer at the Opéra, Rue le Peletier.* Oil on canvas. 1872. Louvre, Paris. Degas became seriously interested in the theatre, as a subject, in the second half of the 1860s. His first pictures were of the orchestra. But it was not long before the theme of the dancer, in performance and in rehearsal, became one of his favorite subjects. In this scene, set in the old Opera House, which was gutted by fire in the autumn of 1873, the ballet master Moraine conducts a class. L. 298.

12. *The Rehearsal.* Oil on canvas. c. 1873. Dumbarton Oaks Research Library and Collection, Washington. Both figures were drawn from the same model, who was probably the artist's sister, Marguerite (1842–1895). The deliberately "untidy" structure of the composition, with a chair occupying the foreground, and a glimpse of ceiling in the top left corner, is intended to emphasize the realistic effect, which is heightened by the deliberately stylized gestures assumed by the women in their rehearsal. L. 331.

13. *Girls Combing their Hair.* *Essense* (i.e., paint diluted with turpentine). 1875–6. Washington, Phillips Collection. Degas sensed that naturalism demanded as much, if not more discipline than classicism; and that the seemingly effortless pose could only be achieved by endless preparatory studies. These he made in oils as well as pastel and pencil. Although vaguely suggestive of a beach scene, this picture is really a study of movement. All three figures are from the same model. L. 376.

14. *Dancer* (detail from *The Rehearsal*). Pastel and gouache. 1875. New York, Private Collection. L. 365.

15. *Women at a Café: Evening.* Pastel over monotype. c. 1877. Louvre, Paris. Shown at the third Impressionist Exhibition, 1877. The scene almost certainly represents prostitutes outside a café on one of the Parisian boulevards. Like Lautrec, Degas was attracted to the theme of prostitution partly because it was a very conspicuous feature of contemporary life, which he wanted to depict in all its aspects. The picture should be compared with a Lautrec such as Plate 64. Note the use of 'vertical piers, which not only contribute to the stability of the design but also, in the way they cut into figures, create a snapshot effect. L. 419.

16. *Café Concert: "The Song of the Dog."* *Essence* and pastel. 1875–7. Horace Havemeyer Collection, New York. Degas's interest in the theatre was not confined to the ballet and legitimate stage. Himself a brilliant mimic, he loved all forms of theatrical impersonation. The café entertainer had the further advantage of representing yet another typical aspect of contemporary life. Degas delighted in the unexpected effect, as in the figure lit from below. Lautrec took over this device from Degas (cf. Plate 59). L. 380.

17. *Harlequin and Colombine.* Pastel on paper. c. 1884. Private Collection. It is interesting to compare Degas's use of the Harlequin figure with that of Cézanne. Cézanne's is essentially a study in structure; Degas's in movement. L. 771.

18. *The Rehearsal.* Oil on canvas. 1873–4. City Museum and Art Gallery, Glasgow. One of the most brilliant of Degas's many studies of the ballet, this painting was seen by the Goncourt brothers when they visited the artist in his studio on the afternoon of Friday the 13th, February, 1874. The dancers did not wear colored sashes at rehearsal; but Degas "introduced" them so as to be able to enliven his scenes with touches of pure color. Several very beautiful pencil studies for this painting survive. L. 430.

19. *Café-Concert des Ambassadeurs*. Pastel over monotype. 1876–7. Musée des Beaux-Arts, Lyons. From the same series as Plate 15, and probably No. 44 in the third Impressionist Exhibition of 1877. L. 405.

20. *L'Absinthe*. Oil on canvas. 1876. Louvre, Paris. Probably shown at the second Impressionist Exhibition in 1876, as *Dans un Café*, *L'Absinthe* represents the actress Ellen Andrée and Marcellin Desboutin, a minor painter of the day, on the terrace of the Café de la Nouvelle-Athènes, which succeeded the Café Guerbois as the favorite Parisian haunt of the Impressionists and their friends. *L'Absinthe* was for some years in England; though it was not then appreciated. When it appeared in an auction at Christie's in 1892, it was hissed, and only fetched £180. Shown at London's Grafton Gallery in March, 1893, it provoked a storm of abuse, being variously described as vulgar, sottish, loathsome, revolting, ugly and degraded. The picture exerted an important influence on Lautrec (cf. Plates 58, 64, 66). L. 393.

21. *Two Laundresses*. *Essence* on paper applied to canvas. 1876–8. Howard H. Sachs Collection, New York. The large, flat areas of color reveal the influence of Japanese prints, which had enjoyed a tremendous vogue among artists since the early 1860s. L. 410.

22. *The Ballet Class*. Oil on canvas. c. 1878. Philadelphia Museum of Art. L. 479.

23. *Dancer on the Stage* (*L'Etoile*). Pastel on paper. 1878. Louvre, Paris. A figure Degas often repeated. See note to Plate 24. L. 491.

24. *The Café Singer*. Pastel. 1878. Fogg Art Museum, Cambridge, Mass. Degas was fascinated by things seen from an unexpected angle. He once planned a series of works illustrating a bakery, "the loaves seen in the cellar or through the air-shafts of the road." In one of his notebooks he decided that "after having made portraits while looking down on the subject, I shall make some looking up. Seated very near a woman and looking from below, I shall see her head in the

chandelier, surrounded by crystals, etc." The unusual viewpoint is a characteristic of Plates 23, 24, 26, 27 and 39. L. 478bis.

25. *The Curtain Falls.* Pastel on board. 1880. Metcalf Collection, Boston. Degas was constantly searching for compositional devices which would enable him to record the momentary act, the aspects of life which remain the same for only a fraction of a second. Cutting the figures with the edge of the descending curtain is a typical, if more than usually bold method. L. 575.

26. *Miss La La at the Cirque Fernando.* Oil on canvas. 1879. National Gallery, London. Miss La La is said to have been a Negress or mulatto who performed feats of strength. The Cirque Fernando, a well known circus in Montmartre, was later a haunt of Toulouse-Lautrec (cf. Plate 54), who greatly admired this painting. L. 522.

27. *Portrait of Diego Martelli.* Oil on canvas. 1879. National Gallery of Scotland, Edinburgh. Diego Martelli (1839–96) was a writer and art critic in Florence, associated with the progressive trends and, after visiting Paris, where he met Degas, one of the first to write in defense of the Impressionists. As in Plate 26, Degas has chosen an unusual viewpoint and the casual effect is enhanced by placing the sitter off center and paying great attention to the papers littering his desk. L. 519.

28. *The Dancer's Dressing Room.* Pastel on paper. 1879. Reinhart Collection, Winterthur. Shown at the fourth Impressionist Exhibition in 1879. Unlike Forain and Lautrec, Degas did not see in the theatrical dressing room an opportunity to present a racy anecdote. The dancer is absorbed in preparing to go on stage. L. 529.

29. *At the Races.* Oil on canvas. 1877–80. Louvre, Paris. The racecourse was always one of Degas's favorite themes. It was a vivid and attractive aspect of contemporary life, and in the jockey he found, as he found in the ballet dancer and the laundress, a subject in which movement naturally played an im-

portant part; and movement which gained in significance because it also represented the exercise of a professional skill. L. 461.

30. *Dancer Leaving her Dressing Room.* Pastel on paper. c. 1881. Niarchos Collection. A work very similar in character to Plate 28. L. 644.

31. *Waiting.* Pastel on paper. c. 1882. Horace Havemeyer Collection, New York. The sheer accuracy of Degas's observation is remarkable. And the figure of the woman in street clothes (perhaps meant to be the dancer's mother), idly tracing patterns on the floor with her umbrella, is one of the artist's most brilliant achievements. Note also the deliberately asymmetrical composition. L. 698.

32. *At the Milliner's.* Oil on canvas. c. 1885. Art Institute of Chicago (Coburn Collection). Degas took up the theme of the hat-shop in the early 1880s, partly as a result of visits he made to fashionable dressmakers with an old friend, Mme. Strauss. L. 832.

33. *After the Bath.* Pastel on paper. 1883. Durand-Ruel Collection, Paris. Shown in the eighth and last Impressionist Exhibition in 1886, as one of a series of studies of the female nude. These received a mixed reception. Some people were shocked by their unidealized character, which was, of course, deliberate. "It is," the artist told George Moore, "the human beast occupied with herself, a cat licking herself." L. 717.

34. *Singer in Green.* Pastel on paper. 1884. Stephen C. Clark Collection, New York. L. 772.

35. *Laundresses.* Oil on canvas. c. 1884. Louvre, Paris. No aspect of life was too humble or too trivial for Degas, who reacted strongly—like the other Impressionists—against the taste of the official Salon. The woman on the left is probably holding a bottle of water for sprinkling, rather than wine for drinking. Another version of this design, in pastel, is in the Norton Simon Collection, Los Angeles. L. 785.

36. *Dancers on Stage, Seen from a Box.* Pastel on paper. 1885. John G. Johnson Collection, Philadelphia. As in Plate 25, Degas exploits an unusual viewpoint to create a spontaneous and vivid effect. Comparison with Plate 57 shows the influence this kind of Degas had on Toulouse-Lautrec. L. 828.

37. *Miss Cassatt at the Louvre.* Pastel on grey paper. 1880. John G. Johnson Collection, Philadelphia. This is a study for a pastel (27 x 20½ in. L. 581), done in 1880 and now in a private collection in New York, showing Mary Cassatt in one of the galleries if the Louvre. Degas told a friend that in these studies, he wanted to suggest the crushed respect and absence of all feeling that women revealed when in the presence of works of art. Mary Cassatt (1845–1926) was an American painter who arrived in Paris in 1874. She became a close friend of Degas and was influenced by his art. L. 582.

38. *Hélène Rouart.* Pastel on paper. Signed and dated 1886. Private Collection, London. One of several studies for a large portrait (L. 869. Oil, 64 x 48⅜ in. René Gimpel Estate) painted in the same year. Hélène Rouart was a daughter of Henri Rouart (1833–1912), who was probably Degas's closest friend. L. 870.

39. *The Tub.* Pastel on paper. 1886. Art Gallery, Farmington, Conn. Like Plate 33, shown at the eighth and last Impressionist Exhibition in 1886. The unusual angle and the impression of a snapshot, with the furniture cut abruptly by the bounding lines of the composition, and which Degas often repeated, influence Toulouse-Lautrec (e.g., Plate 82). L. 876.

40. *Dancers at the Bar.* Oil on canvas. c. 1900–5. Phillips Memorial Gallery, Washington. One of the rare oils from Degas's last years, when he preferred the more manageable medium of pastel. This picture sadly reveals the havoc which the painter's failing sight wrought upon his art. L. 807 (with too early a date).

41. *Dancers in Blue.* Oil on canvas. c. 1890. Louvre, Paris. Degas's

later works became less and less detailed, partly because the artist's great experience enabled him to grasp the essentials of a design, and partly bcause failing sight made it impossible for him to paint with the same minuteness (compare this picture with Plates 11 and 18). L. 1014.

42. *Lake with Mountains.* Pastel. c. 1890–93. Horace Havemeyer Collection, New York. Degas always regarded the human figure as the most important subject for art. His views on landscape were firm: "If I were the government," he once remarked, "I would have a company of police watching out for men who paint landscapes from nature." This did not prevent him, however, from painting nature. In the early 1890s he produced a whole series of pastel scenes like this one. Many of them were shown at Durand-Ruel's in 1893. L. 1048.

43. *Two Dancers.* Pastel on paper. c. 1898. Gallery of Modern Art, Dresden. A design which Degas often repeated. L. 1331.

44. *Horses in Training.* Pastel on paper. c. 1894. Private Collection, New York. L. 1145.

45. *Russian Dancers.* Pastel on paper. 1895. Vollard Collection, Paris. In 1895, a troupe of Russian dancers were performing in national costume at the Folies Bèrgere. The spectacle inspired Degas to make twenty drawings and pastels. L. 1188.

46. *Dancers.* Pastel on paper. c. 1899. Art Gallery, Toledo, Ohio. L. 1344.

47. *Woman Drying Herself.* Pastel on paper. c. 1903. Chicago Art Institute. L. 1426.

48. *Self Portrait*. Oil on board. 1880. Musée Toulouse-Lautrec, Albi. Lautrec shows us his reflection in a mirror, probably placed over a mantelpiece. The originality of the pose and the careful delineation of light and shade reveal Lautrec's innate talent—for at this date he had had no formal training.

49. *The Dog-Cart*. Oil on panel. 1880. Musée Toulouse-Lautrec, Albi. This study reflects the artist's youthful love of the country. After his accident and migration to Paris, however, Lautrec gave up outdoor subjects, using scenery only as a background for his figures.

50. *The Falconer*. Oil on canvas. 1881. Musée Toulouse-Lautrec, Albi. Executed, probably at Céleyran or Le Bosc, in the autumn of 1881, the picture shows the artist's father, Comte Alphonse de Toulouse-Lautrec (1838–1913) setting out on a hunting expedition with one of his falcons. The Comte was extremely eccentric and given to dressing up. He is shown here in a Circassian tunic and turban. Although lively in style, the picture is still very tentative, the structure of the figure, in particular, being weak.

51. *Young Routy*. Oil on canvas. Summer, 1882. Private Collection, Paris. The picture depicts a young farm hand on the Céleyran estate and it reveals the great progress Lautrec had made in the six months he had just spent in Paris, working under Bonnat. The influence of Manet is apparent in the lively intimations of sunlight and air.

52. *"Fat Maria."* Oil on canvas. 1894. Collection of Baron van der Heydt, Ascona, Switzerland. One of the most fundamental differences between Degas and Lautrec was in their attitude toward the model. Degas, even in his most seemingly direct portraits (Plates 5, 9), stresses the individuality of the sitter, but he never becomes personal. In all his work there is an element of discretion and reticence. Lautrec was always bolder and in this respect less sensitive. *"Fat Maria"* has a directness and, in every pucker and fold of the aging body, reveals

an acceptance of—and interest in—the most degrading sides of life. (See also Plates 58, 72, 85.)

53. *Vincent van Gogh*. Pastel. 1887. V. W. van Gogh Collection, Laren, Holland. · Van Gogh reached Paris in March, 1886, but did not get to know Lautrec until the autumn. This portrait, which is in pastel, a medium Lautrec rarely used, was probably painted in the autumn of 1887.

54. *Cirque Fernando: The Equestrienne*. Oil on canvas. 1888. Art Institute of Chicago. This picture is extremely important. It was Lautrec's first serious attempt at a composition with several figures; his first circus scene; and also his first really experimental picture—the emphasis on line and flat pattern at the expense of aerial perspective marking the artist's break with Impressionism. Lautrec was not of course alone in reacting against Impressionist doctrines. In the same year of 1888, for example, Gauguin produced his famous *Vision After the Sermon* (Edinburgh).

55. *The Laundress*. 1889. Collection of Mme. Dortu, Le Vésinet, France. This picture was probably undertaken as an exercise. It should be compared with Degas's treatment of the same theme (Plate 35).

56. *At the Moulin Rouge: The Dance*. Oil on canvas. 1890. Collection of Henry P. McIlhenny, Philadelphia. This is the third of Lautrec's elaborate compositions—the first being Plate 54 and the second *At the Moulin de la Galette* (1889. Chicago Art Institute). The composition, with the rows of figures parallel to the picture plane, is much steadier and combines a lively sense of movement with monumentality of form. The picture includes several portraits of friends of the artist. The two dancers, left center, are Valentin-le-Désossé and La Goulue (see Plates 62 and 76).

57. *At the Nouveau Cirque: Five Stuffed Shirts*. 1891. Philadelphia Museum of Art. This is probably a first idea for a poster which was never produced. It embodies a wry comment on the fashionable audience the Nouveau

Cirque attracted. The sinuous lines of the composition and, in particular, the figure of the dancer anticipate aspects of the Art Nouveau style.

58. *Last Crumbs (À la Mie).* 1891 (February). Museum of Fine Arts, Boston. Shown at the Salon des Indépendants in March, 1891, this study in degradation derives from Degas's *L'Absinthe* (Plate 20). The model for the man was a friend of the painter's called Maurice Guibert. He was a champaigne salesman and Denys Sutton has made the interesting suggestion that the picture may have been meant as some kind of private joke.

59. *At the Moulin Rouge.* 1892. Art Institute of Chicago. The thick rail is used to create a sense of space and the way it is abruptly cut off by the edges of the picture, like the figure of the girl on the right, stresses the spontaneity and effect of immediacy. Once again, the picture contains many portraits of friends of the artist, who put himself in the background, his diminutive stature gleefully contrasted with the lanky figure of his cousin, Gabriel Tapié de Céleyran.

60. *At the Moulin Rouge: Preparing for the Quadrille.* Gouache on board. 1892. National Gallery of Art, Washington (Chester Dale Collection). The *quadrille naturaliste* was a development of the can-can and was performed by dancers in groups of four.

61. *Jane Avril Leaving the Moulin Rouge.* 1892. Wadsworth Atheneum, Hartford. Jane Avril (1868–1943) was a star at the Moulin Rouge in the years 1890–4. She was more refined and altogether more intelligent than the other performers and was perhaps the only one who really appreciated Lautrec's work.

62. *La Goulue Entering the Moulin Rouge.* 1892. Collection of David M. Levy, New York. Louise Weber (1870–1929) started life as a laundry girl in Alsace but after having been brought to Paris in 1886 she became a dancer. Her reign at the Moulin was glorious but brief. She ate far too much (hence *La Goulue*—The Glutton) and by 1895 had grown too fat to perform in Montmartre (see Plate 76).

31

63. *The Ballet "Papa Chrysanthème."* 1892. Musée Toulouse-Lautrec, Albi. *"Papa Chrysanthème,"* an opulent Japanese ballet, was staged at the Nouveau Cirque in November, 1892. The girl on the lotus leaf is performing a veil dance in the style of the current American idol, Loïe Fuller. Lautrec used his sketches of this ballet for a stained-glass window that he designed for Tiffany of New York.

64. *A Corner of a Dance Hall.* Winter of 1892–3. Chester Dale Collection, New York. The picture shows prostitutes on the look-out for customers. The use of the low viewpoint eliminates much of the background, thus concentrating the attention on the figures.

65. *The Kiss.* 1892. Collection of Mme. Dortu, Les Vésinet, France. Lautrec was on friendly terms with the girls and "madames" of the Montmartre brothels and when he accepted a commission to redecorate the salon of an establishment in the Rue d'Amboise he had an opportunity of observing even more closely the girls' habits. Lesbianism, he discovered, was quite common, and he depicted it in the same detached spirit as he showed the man collecting the laundry (Plate 70) or the medical inspection (Plate 72).

66. *M. Boileau in a Café.* 1893 (spring). Cleveland Museum of Art. Virtually nothing is known about the sitter in this portrait, whose design reveals, once again, the influence of Degas's pictures such as *L'Absinthe.*

67. *Jane Avril Dancing.* Oil on board. c. 1893. Niarchos Collection, Paris. This is a preparatory sketch for one of Lautrec's most brilliant posters—*Jane Avril, Jardin de Paris.*

68. *Woman Pulling on her Stockings.* Oil on board. 1894. Musée Toulouse-Lautrec, Albi. A rapid sketch that demonstrates Lautrec's mastery of line.

69. *Yvette Guilbert Taking a Call.* Photographic proof heightened with color. 1894. Musée Toulouse-Lautrec, Albi. Yvette Guilbert (1868–1944),

one of the most celebrated diseuses of the day, came from a bourgeois family. She first appears in Lautrec's work in 1892 (in background of poster *Le Divan Japonais*), but they did not meet until the summer of 1894. Though shocked by the note of caricature, Guilbert was shrewd enough to realize the publicity value of Lautrec's images, by which, in fact, she was best known.

70.   *The Laundryman Calling at the Brothel.*   Oil on board.   1894.   Musée Toulouse-Lautrec, Albi.

71.   *The Salon in the Rue des Moulins.*   Oil on canvas.   1894.   Musée Toulouse-Lautrec, Albi.   Commenced in 1894, but probably not finished until late in 1895, this famous painting represents a summing up of the artist's interest in the *maisons-closes*. Many preparatory drawings exist, and in Albi there is also a large pastel, which the oil painting closely follows. In the use of large simple planes, stress on the silhouette, and restriction of color, the picture reveals the influence of Lautrec's experience as a poster designer.

72.   *Rue des Moulins: the Inspection.*   Oil on board.   1894.   Chester Dale Collection, New York.   Prostitutes in the licensed brothels were subject to regular medical inspections.

73.   *Gabriel Tapié de Céleyran.*   (1869–1930).   Oil on canvas.   1894.   Musée Toulouse-Lautrec, Albi.   Lautrec's cousin, Tapié de Céleyran studied medicine (see Plate 89) and qualified as a doctor. He was devoted to the artist, whose capricious moods and pranks he took in good part. He is shown here strolling in the corridor of a theatre.

74.   *Alfred la Guigne.*   Gouache on board.   1894.   National Gallery of Art, Washington   (Chester Dale Collection). The coat of la Guigne shows how Lautrec would use the color of unprimed board on which he worked as a positive feature in a design.

75.   *Miss May Belfort.*   1895 (spring).   Collection of Leonard C. Hanna Jr.,

New York. May Belfort was an Irish girl who specialized in a pseudo-childish act. Wearing a mob cab tied with a large bow of colored ribbon, and cradling a little black cat in her arms, she would sing sentimental and popular ballads, the piquancy of her act stemming from the often smutty character of her material. Like Degas, Lautrec exploits the striking effect of light illuminating the face from below (cf. Plates 16 and 24).

76. *La Goulue Dancing* (detail). Whole in oil on canvas. 1895. Louvre, Paris. Although now too fat to appear at the Moulin Rouge, "La Goulue" was still able to make some sort of living by touring fairs with a dance act. She asked Lautrec to design two large decorations for the front of her mobile booth; and this is a detail from the right hand panel.

77. *Friends*. Oil on panel. 1895. H. R. Schinz Collection, Zurich. One of several studies of lesbians that Lautrec made in the mid nineties (cf. Plate 65).

78. *Marcelle Lender Dancing the Boléro in "Chilpéric."* Oil on canvas. 1895–6. J. H. Whitney Collection, New York. *Chilpéric* was an operetta by Hervé set—somewhat loosely—in the eighth century. It was revived in Paris in February, 1895, and was a great personal trumph for Marcelle Lender who is here shown, as Galswintha, dancing a boléro before King Chilpéric and the assembled court. Lautrec was fascinated by her performance and person and saw the production over and over again. "I only come to watch Lender's back," he remarked to a friend. "Look at it carefully, for you will never see anything so magnificent."

79. Detail of Plate 78.

80. *At the Moulin Rouge: the Clowness Cha-U-Kao.* Oil on board. 1895. Reinhart Collection, Winterthur. One of the last pictures by Lautrec to be inspired by the Moulin Rouge. The bearded man in a bowler hat on the right is Tristan Bernard, the playwright.

81. *Maxime Dethomas at the Opera Ball.* Gouache on board. 1896. Na-

tional Gallery of Art, Washington (Chester Dale Collection). Dethomas (1868–1928) was a painter and engraver, and one of Lautrec's closest friends from the early nineties until his death.

82. *Woman at her Toilet.* Oil on board. 1896. Louvre, Paris. One of Lautrec's most technically accomplished pictures, this study reveals, once again, the influence of Degas in the unexpected angle (cf. Plate 39).

83. *A Box at the Theatre.* Oil on board. Winter of 1896–7. Hans Metter Collection, St. Gallen, Switzerland. The use of a strong diagonal, to create a sense of space, had been adopted by Lautrec before (see Plate 59); but here the effect is more monumental. The man in the background is Tom, a Rothschild coachman. The woman in a rather masculine outfit in the foreground is Mme. Armande Brazier, a one-eyed ex-prostitute who became the proprietress of *Le Hanneton,* a well known lesbian haunt in Montmartre.

84. *Portrait of Berthe Bady.* Oil on board. 1897. Musée Toulouse-Lautrec, Albi. Mlle. Bady was one of the leading actresses at the Théâtre de l'Oeuvre, which had been founded in 1893 by Lugné-Poë, a friend of Lautrec. The theatre specialized in Symbolist Drama.

85. *Nude in Front of a Mirror.* Oil on board. 1897. Collection of Mr. and Mrs. Ira Haupt, New York. In the late nineties, Lautrec's style began to change. He placed less emphasis on line, and more on modelling in planes, and his coloring became darker and richer. This is one of the artist's most uncompromising studies of the nude.

86. *In a Private Room at the Rat Mort.* Oil on canvas. 1899. Courtauld Gallery, London. Early in 1899, Lautrec suffered a complete mental and nervous collapse and was confined to a sanitarium, where he remained under treatment until May. This is one of the pictures he produced soon after his release. Like Plate 85, it is in a more painterly style than his earlier work. This development cannot be dissociated from the state of Lautrec's health. Linear precision must

have become much more difficult as the late nights, bouts of drinking and sexual excess began to take their toll. The present picture shows Lucy Jourdan, a well-known *demi-mondaine,* dining at the *Rat Mort,* which was a fashionable restaurant in the rue Pigalle. It is said to have been commissioned by her lover, a certain Baron de W.

87. *The Barmaid.* Oil on panel. 1899. Musée Toulouse-Lautrec, Albi. After leaving the sanitarium, Lautrec went on a tour, which soon degenerated into a spree. While at Le Havre in July (1899), he made many sketches at The Star, a noisy bar frequented by the English sailors. One of the best of his late works, this is a study of an English barmaid who worked there.

88. *Woman at her Toilet: Mme Poupoule.* Oil on panel. Musée Toulouse-Lautrec, Albi. 1900 (?) Generally dated 1898; but Douglas Cooper has given convincing reasons for a slightly later dating. The coloring in this study is subdued and the mood forlorn.

89. *An Examination at the Faculty of Medicine, Paris.* Oil on canvas. 1901. Musée Toulouse-Lautrec, Albi. Lautrec's last painting, on which he was working up to his death. The style, which is very free, betrays definite signs of the artist's physical exhaustion. The picture shows Professor Robert Wurtz examining Gabriel Tapié de Céleyran on his doctoral thesis, which he had submitted in 1899.

90. "Messalina." 38½ x 31 in. 1900–1901. Collection of Henry Pearlman, New York. In December, 1900, Lautrec moved to Bordeaux, where he took a studio. His interest in the theatre was as keen as ever and he set about making a series of paintings of *Messalina,* a new operetta by Isidore de Lara in which the leading role was taken by a Mlle. Ganne.

THE PLATES

1 Degas: *Self Portrait in a Green Vest*.   c. 1855-6.   Oil.   15¾ × 12¼ in.   Nepveu-Degas Collection.   The essential Degas, aloof, quizzical and unromantic.

2 Degas: *Still-Life*.   c. 1858–60.   Oil on paper applied to canvas. 7¼ × 5¾ in.   Private Collection, New York.   One of Degas's rare still-lifes.

3 Degas: *The Young Spartans*. 1860. Oil on canvas. 43 × 61 in. National Gallery, London.
There is very little archaeological detail in this history picture.

4 Degas: *The Bellelli Family*. c. 1858–62. Oil on canvas. 80 × 101 in. Louvre, Paris. The artist's aunt, uncle and cousins are shown in their sitting room.

5 Degas: *Thérèse de Gas.* c. 1863. Oil on canvas. 35 × 23¼ in. Louvre, Paris. Thérèse was the painter's younger sister.

6 Degas: *Study of a Young Woman*.   c. 1867.   Oil on canvas.   10¾ × 8¾ in.   Louvre, Paris.
The interest in forms as they appear under light is characteristically Impressionist.

7 Degas: *Study of Hands.* c. **1858–62.** Oil on canvas. **15¼ × 18½** in. Louvre, Paris. Degas was one of the greatest draughtsmen of the century.

8 Degas: *Auguste de Gas Listening to Pagans.*   c. 1869–72.   Oil on canvas.   32 × 25¼ in.
Museum of Fine Arts, Boston.   Degas inherited a love of music from his father.

9 Degas: *Hortense Valpinçon*. c. 1870. Oil on canvas. 29¾ × 44¾ in. Minneapolis Institute of Fine Arts. An interrupted action is shown.

10 Degas: *Carriage at the Races.* c. 1870–73. Oil on canvas. 14⅛ × 21⅝ in. Museum of Fine Arts, Boston. The abruptly cut edges increase the "snapshot" effect.

11 Degas: *The Dance Foyer at the Opéra, Rue le Peletier*. 1872. Oil on canvas. 12⅞ × 18½ in.
Louvre, Paris. The theatre, as a subject, began to interest Degas in the second half of the 1860s.

12 Degas: *The Rehearsal.* c. 1873. Oil on canvas. 31⅞ × 25⅝ in. Dumbarton Oaks Research Library and Collection, Washington. Both figures were drawn from the same model.

13 Degas: *Girls Combing their Hair.* 1875–6. Essence (paint diluted with turpentine). 13½ × 18½ in. Phillips Collection, Washington. A brilliant study of gesture and movement.

14 Degas: *Dancer* (detail from *The Rehearsal*). 1875–6. Pastel and gouache. 22 × 27 in.
Private Collection, New York. Degas is the greatest of all painters of the dance.

15 Degas: *Women at a Café: Evening.*   c. 1877.   Pastel over monotype.   16 × 25⅝ in.
Louvre, Paris.   The girls are prostitutes—Degas wanted to depict life in all its aspects.

16 Degas: *Café Concert: "The Song of the Dog."* c. 1875–7. 21⅝ × 17¾ in. Essence and pastel. Horace Havemeyer Col., N.Y. Degas loved all forms of theatrical impersonation.

17 Degas: *Harlequin and Colombine*.   c. 1884.   Pastel on paper.   16½ × 16½ in.   Private
Collection.   The suggestion of movement is powerfully conveyed.

18 Degas: *The Rehearsal*. 1873–4. Oil on canvas. 23 × 33 in. City Museum and Art Gallery, Glasgow. Several pencil studies for this painting survive.

19 Degas: *Café-Concert des Ambassadeurs*. c. 1876–7. Oil on canvas. 14¾ × 10¾ in. Musée des Beaux Arts, Lyons. Degas delighted in the unexpected angle of sight.

20 Degas: *L'Absinthe*. 1876. Oil on canvas. 37 × 27½ in. Louvre, Paris. This famous picture was sold in London for £180.

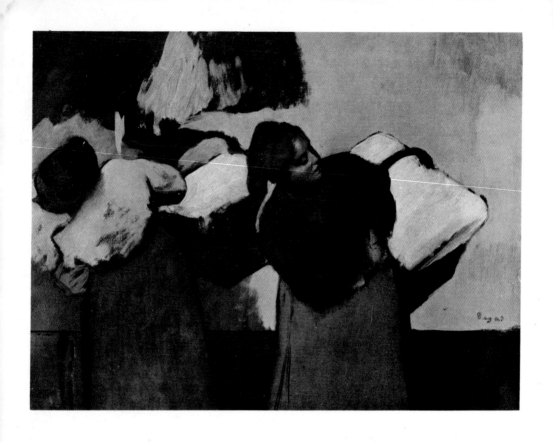

21 Degas: *Two Laundresses*.   1876–8.   Essence on paper applied to canvas.   18 × 24 in.   Howard
H. Sachs Col., New York.   The large flat areas reveal the influence of Japanese prints.

22 Degas: *The Ballet Class.* c. 1878. Oil on canvas. 32½ × 30½ in. Philadelphia Museum of Art. The sashes, not worn at rehearsal, were "introduced" by Degas to add color.

23 Degas: *Dancer on the Stage (L'Etoile)*. 1878. Pastel on paper. 24 × 17½ in. Louvre,
Paris. Degas often repeated figures in slightly different compositions.

24 Degas: *The Café Singer*.   1878.   Pastel.   21¼ × 16½ in.   Fogg Art Museum, Cambridge.
The bold use of the head in close-up was another device taken over from Japanese prints.

25 Degas: *The Curtain Falls*.   1880.   Pastel on board.   21¾ × 29¾ in.   Metcalf Collection, Boston.   An unusually bold composition.

26 Degas: *Miss La La at the Cirque Fernando*. 1879. Oil on canvas. 46 × 30½ in. National Gallery, London. Degas admired professional skills, and often recorded them.

27 Degas: *Portrait of Diego Martelli.* 1879. Oil on canvas. 43½ × 39¾ in. National Gallery of Scotland, Edinburgh. Martelli was a critic and writer from Florence.

28 Degas: *The Dancer's Dressing Room.* 1879. Pastel on paper. 24 × 17¼ in. Reinhart Collection, Winterthur. The glimpse through the open door enhances the sense of ordinary life.

29 Degas: *At the Races*. c. 1877–80. Oil on canvas. 26½ × 32¾ in. Louvre, Paris. The asymmetry of this composition is particularly marked.

30 Degas: *Dancer Leaving her Dressing Room.* c. 1881. Pastel on paper. 20¾ × 12½ in.
Niarchos Collection. As his eyesight deteriorated, he relied increasingly upon pastels.

31 Degas: *Waiting*. c. 1882. Pastel on paper. 18½ × 23⅝ in. Horace Havemeyer Collection, New York. Among Degas's most penetrating studies of the human figure.

32 Degas: *At the Milliner's.* c. 1885. Oil on canvas. 39⅝ × 43⅝ in. Coburn Collection, Art Institute of Chicago. The elaborate hat permits the use of bold colors.

33 Degas: *After the Bath*. 1883. Pastel on paper. 21¼ × 13¼ in. Durand-Ruel Collection, Paris. Degas abandoned the traditional treatment of the nude as sensuous spectacle.

34 Degas: *Singer in Green.* 1884. Pastel on paper. 24 × 18 in. Stephen C. Clark Col., N.Y. Degas was always interested in curious natural effects—here, the light cast upward on the singer.

35 Degas: *Laundresses*. c. 1884. Oil on canvas. 29⅞ × 32¼ in. Louvre, Paris. Weariness is strongly suggested in the attitudes of these two laundresses.

36   Degas: *Dancers on Stage: Seen from a Box*.   1885.   Pastel on paper.   25⅝ × 19⅝ in.   John G. Johnson Collection, Philadelphia.   The view is from a side box.

37 Degas: *Miss Cassatt at the Louvre*. 1880. Pastel on grey paper. 24 × 18½ in. John G. Johnson Collection, Philadelphia. The American painter Mary Cassatt was a close friend.

38 Degas: *Hélène Rouart*. Signed and dated 1886. Pastel on paper. 19¼ × 12½ in. Private
Collection, London. The daughter of the artist's old friend Henri Rouart.

39 Degas: *The Tub*. 1886. Pastel on paper. 28 × 28 in. Art Gallery, Farmington. Degas's women undress not for our admiration, but to wash themselves.

40 Degas: *Dancers at the Bar*. c. 1900–05. Oil on canvas. 51 × 38 in. Phillips Memorial Gallery, Washington. Degas regularly attended dance rehearsals.

41 Degas: *Dancers in Blue*. c. 1890. Oil on canvas. 34 × 30 in. Louvre, Paris. His later works become less and less detailed.

42 Degas: *Lake with Mountains.* c. 1890–93. Pastel. 10 × 13¾ in. Horace Havemeyer Collection, New York. Pure landscape is a rarity in Degas's work.

43 Degas: *Two Dancers*. 1898. Pastel on paper. 39¼ × 35½ in. Gallery of Modern Art, Dresden. This is a design that Degas often repeated.

44 Degas: *Horses in Training.* c. 1894. Pastel on paper. 19¼ × 25½ in. Private Collection, New
York. Many of the later pictures were painted in the studio from memory.

45 Degas: *Russian Dancers*. 1895. Pastel on paper. 19¼ × 26¾ in. Vollard Collection, Paris. These Russian dancers appeared in national costume at the Folies-Bergère.

46 Degas: *Dancers*. c. 1889. Pastel on paper. 24½ × 25½ in. Art Gallery, Toledo, Ohio. Long experience enabled him to suggest essentials of movement without describing forms in detail.

47 Degas: *Woman Drying Herself.* c. 1903. Pastel on paper. 28 × 29¼ in. Art Institute of Chicago. Many of the late works are anti-naturalistic in their coloring.

48 Lautrec: *Self Portrait*. 1880. Oil on board. 15⅞ × 12¾ in. Musée Toulouse-Lautrec, Albi. Done at the age of sixteen before any formal training.

49 Lautrec: *The Dog Cart*. 1880. Oil on panel. 10⅝ × 14¾ in. Musée Toulouse-Lautrec, Albi.
Lautrec's youthful love of horses is expressed in his subject matter.

50 Lautrec: *The Falconer*. 1881. Oil on canvas. 9½ × 5½ in. Musée Toulouse-Lautrec, Albi.
A study of the artist's extremely eccentric father.

51 Lautrec: *Young Routy*. 1882. Oil on canvas. 23⅝ × 19¼ in. Private Collection, Paris. The
keen interest in the fall of light reflects Impressionist influence.

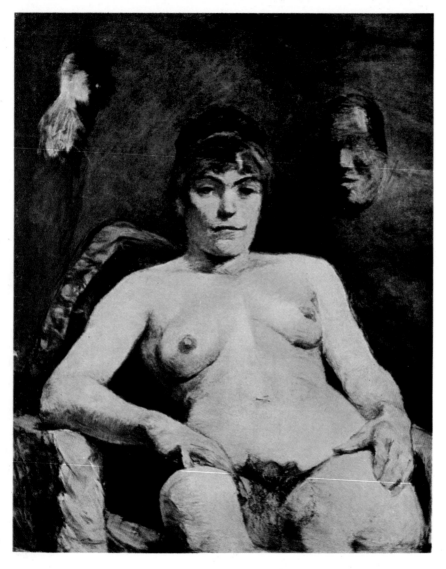

52 Lautrec: *"Fat Maria."* 1884. Oil on canvas. 31½ × 25⅝ in. Col. of Baron van der Heydt, Ascona, Switzerland. Lautrec does not conceal the model's physical and moral decay.

53 Lautrec: *Vincent van Gogh*. 1887. Pastel. 22½ × 18½ in. V. W. Van Gogh Collection, Laren, Holland. Lautrec and Van Gogh knew each other briefly in the mid-1880s.

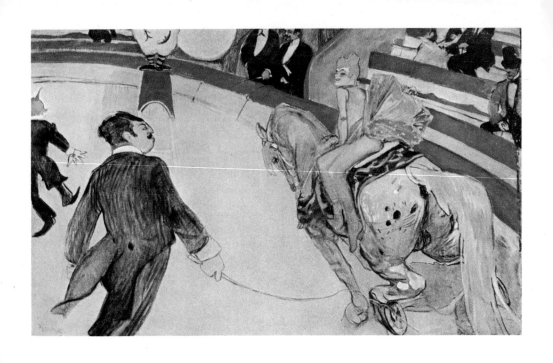

54 Lautrec: *Cirque Fernando: The Equestrienne.* 1888. Oil on canvas. 38¾ × 63½ in. Art Institute of Chicago. His emphasis on line, flat pattern, and bold color emerges here.

55 Lautrec: *The Laundress.* 1889. 36⅝ × 29½ in. Collection of Mme. Dortu, Le Vésinet, France. This study shows that Lautrec could produce excellent traditional work.

56 Lautrec: *At the Moulin Rouge: The Dance*. 1890. Oil on canvas. 45 × 59 in. Collection of Henry P. McIlhenny, Philadelphia. The Moulin Rouge inspired some of his most popular works.

57 Lautrec: *At the Nouveau Cirque: Five Stuffed Shirts*. 1891. 23⅝ × 15¾ in. Philadelphia Museum of Art. His use of line was more exaggerated and decorative than Degas's.

58 Lautrec: *Last Crumbs (À la Mie)*. 1891. 19¾ × 27½ in. Museum of Fine Arts, Boston. A study in degradation that may have been intended as a joke.

59   Lautrec: *At the Moulin Rouge.* 1892. 47½ × 55¼ in. Art Institute of Chicago. Portraits of many of the artist's friends are included here.

60 Lautrec: *At the Moulin Rouge: Preparing for the Quadrille*. 1892. Gouache on board.
31½ × 23¾ in. National Gallery, Washington. The dance here was a variety of the can-can.

61 Lautrec: *Jane Avril Leaving the Moulin Rouge*. 1892. 33⅞ × 25½ in. Wadsworth Atheneum,
Hartford. The unusual color combinations give this study a haunting poetry.

62 Lautrec: *La Goulue Entering the Moulin Rouge.* 1892. 31½ × 23 in. Col. of David M. Levy, N.Y. A wry study of the ex-laundry girl who became a brief Moulin Rouge idol.

63 Lautrec: *The Ballet "Papa Chrysanthème."* 1892. 23¼ × 31⅛ in. Musée Toulouse-Lautrec Albi. The Japanese influence is strong here in both subject and treatment.

64 Lautrec: *A Corner of the Dance Hall.* 1892–3. 40 × 39 in. Chester Dale Collection, Washington. A dwarf and alcoholic, Lautrec had few illusions about human nature.

65 Lautrec: *The Kiss*. 1892. 15⅜ × 22⅞ in. Col. of Mme. Dortu, Les Vésinet, France. The artist's detachment removes any possibility of obscenity.

66 Lautrec: *M. Boileau in a Café.* 1893. 31½ × 25⅝ in. Cleveland Museum of Art. Lautrec was at his best with themes of urban pleasure.

67 Lautrec: *Jane Avril Dancing.* c. 1893. Oil on board. 39 × 28½ in. Niarchos Collection, Paris. Lautrec was among the first and the greatest of poster designers.

68   Lautrec: *Woman Pulling on her Stockings.* 1894. Oil on board. 23⅝ × 17 in. Musée Toulouse-Lautrec, Albi. Lautrec was somewhat superficial compared to Degas. (See Plates 33, 39.)

69 Lautrec: *Yvette Guilbert Taking a Call.* Photographic proof heightened with color. **18⅞ ×
9⅞** in. Musée Toulouse-Lautrec, Albi. An elegantly wicked study.

70 Lautrec: *Laundryman Calling at the Brothel*. 1894. Oil on board. 26⅜ × 17¾ in. Musée Toulouse-Lautrec, Albi. The reactions of respectable people always amused Lautrec.

71 Lautrec: *The Salon in the Rue des Moulins.* 1894. Oil on canvas. 43⅞ × 52⅛ in. Musée Toulouse-Lautrec, Albi. Few artists have treated the subject so unlasciviously.

72 Lautrec: *Rue des Moulins: The Inspection.* 1894. Oil on board. 31¾ × 21¾ in. Chester Dale Col., Washington. Nothing was too sacred—or too trivial—for Lautrec's mordant eye.

73 Lautrec: *Gabriel Tapié de Céleyran* (1869–1930). 1894. Oil on canvas. 43¼ × 22 in. Musée Toulouse-Lautrec, Albi. A charming study of the artist's lanky cousin.

74 Lautrec: *Alfred la Guigne*. 1894. Gouache on board. 25¾ × 19¾ in. National Gallery, Washington. The color of the unprimed board becomes the color of la Guigne's coat.

75 Lautrec: *Miss May Belfort*. 1895. 31½ × 23⅝ in. Col. of Leonard C. Hanna Jr., New York.
May Belfort was a great success singing smutty songs while dressed as a child.

76 Lautrec: *La Goulue Dancing* (detail). 1895. Whole in oil on canvas. 114 × 124 in. Louvre, Paris. One of two decorations made for the front of a mobile booth.

77 Lautrec: *Friends*. 1895. Oil on panel. 17¾ × 26⅜ in. H. R. Schinz Col., Zurich. A deformed outcast, Lautrec had a tender regard for genuine affection of any kind.

78 Lautrec: *Marcelle Lender Dancing the Boléro in "Chilpéric."* 1895-6. Oil on canvas. 57⅛ × 59 in. J. H. Whitney Col., N.Y. Lautrec saw the opera repeatedly, fascinated by the dancer.
79 (Overleaf) Detail of Plate 78.

80 Lautrec: *At the Moulin Rouge: The Clowness Cha-U-Kao.* 1895. Oil on board. 29½ × 21⅜ in. Reinhart Col., Winterthur. An irretrievable sadness amid the gaiety.

81 Lautrec: *Maxime Dethomas at the Opera Ball.* 1896. Gouache on board. 26½ × 21 in. National Gallery of Art, Washington. Dethomas was one of the artist's closest friends.

82 Lautrec: *Woman at her Toilet*. 1896. Oil on board. 25⅝ × 20⅞ in. Louvre, Paris. Very close in spirit to the work of Degas.

83 Lautrec: *A Box at the Theatre*. 1896–7. Oil on board. 21⅝ × 18½ in. Hans Metter Col., St. Gallen, Switzerland. The lines of the box are an integral part of the design.

84 Lautrec: *Portrait of Berthe Bady*. 1897. Oil on board. 27⅛ × 22⅞ in. Musée Toulouse-Lautrec, Albi. One of Lautrec's straightforward portraits.

85 Lautrec: *Nude in Front of a Mirror.* 1897. Oil on board. 24¾ × 18⅞ in. Col. of Mr. and Mrs. Ira Haupt, New York. One of the artist's most uncompromising nude studies.

86   Lautrec: *In a Private Room at the Rat Mort*. 1899. Oil on canvas. 21½ × 17¾ in. Courtauld Gallery, London. The unusual lighting heightens this study of *la dolce vita*.

87 Lautrec: *The Barmaid*. 1899. Oil on panel. 16⅛ × 12⅞ in. Musée Toulouse-Lautrec, Albi.
One of the best of Lautrec's later works, done after leaving the sanatorium.

88　Lautrec: *Woman at her Toilet: Mme. Poupoule*.　1900?.　Oil on panel.　23⅝ × 15¾ in.　Musée Toulouse-Lautrec, Albi.　The forlorn mood is represented by the drab coloring.

89 Lautrec: *An Examination at the Faculty of Medicine, Paris.* 1901. Oil on canvas. **24¾** × **31⅛** in. Musée Toulouse-Lautrec, Albi. This is Lautrec's last picture.

90 Lautrec: *"Messalina."* 1900–01. 38½ × 31 in. Collection of Henry Pearlman, New York. Lautrec's later paintings are much less incisively drawn.